A TALE OF MAGICIANS WHO PUFFED UP MONEY THAT LOST ITS PUFF

twenty or so poems & a magic show

KAIA SAND

Many of these poems have been cast in social
spaces—as paper airplanes tossed in Cabaret
Voltaire, flowers handed out next to a farmers'
market, lines embroidered on a dropcloth
and on linen swaying in the window, lines
reverberated through the people's microphone
at Occupy Portland, a magic show.

Kaia Sand is the the author of *Remember to Wave*
(Tinfish Press 2010), and *interval* (Edge Books
2004), *a Small Press Traffic Book of the Year,* and she
co-authored *Landscapes of Dissent: Guerrilla Poetry and
Public Space* (Palm Press 2008) with Jules Boykoff.
She documents her investigative poetry projects and
installations at http://kaiasand.net/

A TALE OF MAGICIANS
WHO PUFFED UP MONEY
THAT LOST ITS PUFF
by Kaia Sand
Copyright © 2016 | All rights reserved
ISBN-13: 978-0-9891861-8-6

Tinfish Press is a 501(c)3 non-profit, tax-exempt cor-
poration that supports the publication of experimental
poetry from the Pacific. Tinfish books are available
from Small Press Distribution in Berkeley, California
(spdbooks.org) and from our website.

TINFISH PRESS
Susan M. Schultz, Editor
47-728 Hui Kelu St. #9
Kāne'ohe, Hi. 96744
press.tinfish@gmail.com

Designed by Jeff Sanner

Support from the John Wythe White & Victoria ail-
White's Left Wing Right Brain Fund of the Hawai'i
Community Foundation.

www.tinfishpress.com

I
THE PRESIDENT
PROBABLY TALKS
AIR THE FIRE
SO HE RAISED
HIS HAND

THE PRESIDENT PROBABLY TALKS

the president probably talks to someone every day

sometimes his lips are moving, but our volume's too low

sometimes his voice is a tenth the volume of mine

sometimes his voice trembles inside my ten voices

sometimes his ten words devalue the currency

sometimes we promise

sometimes someone looks into someone's eyes for truth

sometimes we think we see it

in someone's ten coughs, tuberculosis is passed from cot to cot

sometimes ten walls separate me from two people making one decision somewhere somehow ten women join ten women join ten women and march

my ten voices are still talking

somewhere in this city, ten meals in ten days is a boon

sometimes senators dine together

sometimes ten layoffs boom the business

sometimes we promise our poor

sometimes I feel like a holy-ten-voice-roller

in some sudden kiss, courage intensifies ten-fold

sometimes ten men join ten women join tens and tens and tens

sometimes someone somewhere somehow hears this

AIR THE FIRE
A TRIPTYCH

THE BRIGHT THREAT
OF ATTENTION

Where is anonymity within a public document—
a woman photographed on a porch, her face draped by bangs
faces shaded in prints exposed to scant light
faces shrouded by waterspots
Among throngs of demands for justice
faces blocked by banners
crowds mounding into anonymity
      But your face!
        your face exposed
        to the bright threat of attention

SUREFIRE GLARE
OF RECOGNITION

Where is anonymity within a public document—
a flag of ink blotting out a name
jottings smeared on a dashed-off note
a photograph tagged to the wrong name
rollcall eavesdropped with a tin ear
a pseudonym signed by hand
faints names on a weathered petition
       But in the surefire
       glare of recognition
       —your name

AFIRE WITH
PURPOSE

In the bright threat of attention
the surefire glare of recognition
you became a public person
mindful of those who live
downriver and downwind
from the malice of power
downtrodden by disregard
upbraided by rancor
       For them, you—
       heart-sure, afire
       with purpose—
       you became a public person

SO HE
RAISED
HIS
HAND

WITH LLOYD MARBET

HAND

‘YOU MAY LIVE HERE UNDER TWO CONDITIONS. EVERYTHING YOU OWN MUST BE ON WHEELS & YOU MUST CONTINUE TO DO YOUR ACTIVISM’

With that, Earl the signmaker, the draftsman, the conscientious objector, Earl the landowner who loved trees made Lloyd the Caretaker of these wetlands. This cedar, hawthorne, trillium, douglas fir, these fern, nettles. One who takes care, who cares, who is cared for —

cared for by the woman who stitched him a suit, cared for by the man who loaned a typewriter, cared for by the woman who led walks into the woods of all the people who cared, all the people gathering, with the man who takes care

It was 1969 when the Caretaker drove into Hood River & met an old man who sold plums, a man who could neither read nor write, a man who knew how to grow & love his plum trees

The Caretaker wanted to be like that old man then, & now

he walks through his small orchard: red currants, cherry, cherry, plum, plum, cherry, cherry, cherry, plum. Coffee grounds heaped on the soil. Trees singing with chimes.

It was 1969 when he drove over Mt. Hood & stayed —

Diane brought home
The Perils of the Peaceful Atom
by Elizabeth Hogan & Richard Curtis

Here we were bringing new life
into this world—our daughter
had not yet been born—& I
didn't have a critical awareness
about nuclear power

I'll never forget—
I was sitting at a table
in this shotgun house
we were living in
on 54th & Steele
in SE Portland, &

I got about five chapters into this book when

I suggested we move to Canada

if PGE built Trojan

Yes—
that's what we ought to do said Diane

I turned the page

& the title of the next chapter was

'Don't Bother Running'

I was a rat in a corner

I'd been halfway
around the world

drove boats for the war
in Vietnam
but only just then
while reading this book
did I realize

that, by god   the Earth really was a closed life support system

There was no going to Canada   Canada wasn't going to escape
what happened if Trojan melted down

The only thing I had left
was to find out if it was true   I started going
to the library

educating myself about nuclear power
then I picked up the habit
of going to public hearings   It seemed a good place
to share these concerns

HE HAD TO
SEE IF IT WAS TRUE
HE HAD TO SEE IF IT WAS TRUE
SO HE READ SOME BOOKS
& READ SOME MORE
HE HAD TO CHANGE WAS IT
WAS HE KNEW

PGE decided to build a new nuclear plant   after Trojan

there were all kinds of ideas cooking
on the burners of these utilities
          about future energy demands   they projected
                                                         we'd need 20
                                                         nuclear plants
                                                         in the Pacific
                                                         Northwest

So I show up   at a state licensing hearing for the
                    proposed Boardman Nuclear Plant & the hearing officer
                         asks who's here that wants to intervene

I'm looking around   waiting   for someone
                                        to raise their hand
                                          but nobody did
                                        So I raised my hand
thinking I'll later find someone else
to take my place   I handwrote a petition to intervene

          then went to find the lawyers who had challenged Trojan
                    but they were tired & worn down

                                        I wondered what the hell
                                          I was going to do

I got a notice to show up at an elementary school   I didn't even own a car
     in Boardman for the evidentiary hearing   so I bought a Greyhound ticket
                                                            but I was so flustered
                                                           by everything that I got
                                                             the date wrong & arrived
                                                           the day before the hearing
I slept that night on a beach   was to take place
by the Columbia River   showed up at the hearing
                                    disheveled as hell &
                                    feeling a whole bunch of fear

They started the hearing and got to the point where they were to decide
if I could intervene, & just then all my fear overran me

               "I can't do this." "Are you sure, Mr. Marbet?"
               I just felt like I didn't know what I was doing

They happily dismissed my application

SO HE RAISED HIS HAND
FEELING A WHOLE
BUNCH OF FEAR

SO HE RAISED HIS HAND
& HE NEVER QUIT AFTER THAT

I was sitting in the audience
watching the hearing proceed without me

& feeling ashamed of myself
feeling like I had betrayed
the concerns growing inside me

What happened next was a great unforeseen miracle

PGE had proposed building this nuclear
plant next to a naval bombing range

Even though they were all saying at the time
nuclear plants could withstand anything

the Siting Council decided
that accidentally bombing a nuclear plant   could be a problem

So they announced that same day
they weren't going to let that happen

Bam!   Just like that.   The hearing was over!

PGE reapplied to build the Pebble Springs nuclear plant 25 miles away
in Arlington, & I was honing my typing skills, & I made my next petition
to intervene in the Pebble Springs licensing hearings

I never quit after that!

I taught myself administrative law
I learned to make motions
I learned to do legal research

Utility lawyers are like rare butterflies

Public citizens can't afford
rare butterflies

So I made myself   into another kind
of rare butterfly:

a citizen intervener

THE TRILLIUM PURPLES
ITS WHITE LEAVES
AS SUMMER DEEPENS ITS SEASON
& HE BECAME A PUBLIC PERSON

& HE BECAME A PUBLIC PERSON

PGE built a fancy road to the nuclear plant they hadn't even built

They were pouring money into the community

& the people loved it

They said they had been in
the Depression since the Depression

& they felt very threatened
by us because they saw us
as obstructionists

I understood their plight
The last thing I wanted
was for the people of Arlington
to remain in the Depression

but there had to be a better way out

than buying into this
unproven
dangerous
technology

Three-Mile Island   Chernobyl   Fukushima

I'm not arrogant enough to think I'm right all the time
But say Pebble Springs was built & we had our own nuclear meltdown

The community wouldn't have been able to go home
just like Chernobyl
I recently had surgery for cancer & my doctor told me about
three Russian patients he had who all have bladder cancer
So my doctor decides to ask them
if they had been at Chernobyl
during the accident
Yes, they had
been at Chernobyl

Last year I was driving the Gorge along those roads I drove so often
to the Pebble Springs hearings, & for 40 miles I didn't lose sight
of those big wind generators   Jesus, it blew me away

all those wind generators
near the road
to the nuclear plant   that never got built

NOW GO FOLLOW THAT ROAD
NOW GO FOLLOW THAT ROAD

& RECALL DOWN THAT ROAD
WHAT NEVER CAME TO BE

We'd just lost our third ballot measure to shut Trojan down
when someone at the Nuclear Regulatory Commission

        leaked a report   to Robert Pollard at
                the Union of Concerned Scientists

the report, written by NRC scientists, declared
    Trojan unsafe to operate

           The steam generators were failing

          I mean, it was like Trojan was slated
             to become a disaster

    They had engineers
    building that nuclear plant
     who had never even
      built a wall &   the steam generators came with
              a thirty-day warranty

but the Nuclear Regulatory Commission
      —which had been rubberstamping
         nuclear plants since day one—
                suppressed
When Pollard released it   the study
   we decided to petition the government
    to hold new hearings on
   whether it was safe to operate Trojan

        So we petitioned everyone
        & they all said no
   There were many forms of protest against Trojan
& I did petitions & licensing proceedings

           I wanted to exhaust
       all the avenues
          before I tried
     Civil Disobedience
   But when they turned us down
  for a hearing on safety   there was no alternative left

That December, in 1992, we went to the gates of Trojan
to stop the workers from coming into the plant

           We felt justified
        to stand at those gates

THEY STOOD AT THE GATES
& THEY STOOD AT THE GATES

IT SEEMED THE PLACE
TO SHARE THESE CONCERNS
& THEY NEVER QUIT AFTER THAT

We ended up on trial
after spending weeks
in jail for blocking
the gates of Trojan
The state finally decided they had to hold a hearing
over Trojan's safety & then PGE immediately decided it was time
to permanently close Trojan down

but that corporation was not without its vindictiveness
It still went forward with its criminal charges against us

So we raised a choice of evils defense:
Say you see a house is burning down
You decide to bust the door down
in case someone is trapped inside

You've broken the law

but the hazardousness of the situation   supersedes the law

That's a choice of evils defense   &, lo & behold

the judge allowed us
to raise this defense   so we moved to have access
to PGE's files
We wanted everything they had
on the steam generators

the moment the judge granted our motion to see this evidence
the utility attorney whispered
in the ear of the prosecuting attorney
who then stood up to announce
they were dropping all of the charges against us

It was a great disappointment!
The people of Oregon deserved to see those documents
Now there was no way that could happen
& before PGE even made a decommissioning plan
they filled the broken
steam generators with concrete
barged them upriver
to Hanford   & buried them   in a hole
in the ground

O THEY SUNK THE EVIDENCE OF
WHAT WENT WRONG

O SOME WHO CARE GATHER
CROWDS INTO SONG

Every time we lost
Every time we lost

EVERY TIME THEY LOST

You would think losing
is such a heavy thing

When I first started petitioning   someone spit in my face

I remember thinking at the time
I'm never going to go out
& get another signature   boy, was I wrong about that

We'd get the signatures, run the campaigns

but all PGE's money would overwash us

They broke
every spending record
in every election
we put them through

Three different elections we tried
to close Trojan down & they beat us

they beat us down
into the ground

but we always rose from the ashes

We kept coming back

over &
over

It was finally at a PGE board meeting when they shut Trojan down
I'm willing to bet they knew the Trojan Decommissioning Alliance
was out there. They knew the Coalition for Safe Power was out there
Don't Waste Oregon—
They knew we were all still out there &

They knew we'd be back

& we would become

more powerful than before

EVERY TIME THEY LOST

EVERY TIME THEY LOST

EVERY TIME THEY LOST

EVERY TIME MORE

POWERFUL THAN BEFORE

The Caretaker walks past a mossy-topped
mailtruck packed with rafting gear, past sunning
garter snakes

He walks past a small trailer lined with the sweet
wood air of cedar scavenged from the ruins of a
shopping center that he & his son
handwashed

He walks over mud-rutted trails compacted with dirt
beneath wood chips flung on filter fabric

He walks past twinned douglas firs a treehouse-width
apart, says he longs to live up there
not in quick shelter, but in the sky—

but he leaves the tree be, stays grounded

Caring. Showing up

II

Inhale, exhale

7.4 billion people breathing

Some of us in captivity

Our crops far-flung

Prison is a place where children sometimes visit

Jetted from Japan, edamame is eaten in England

Airplane air is hard to share

 KAIA SAND

I breathe in what you breathe out, stranger

Tantalum is mined by hand for cell phones

Sometimes children dig it

We send tea leaves to distant friends

Neighbors bike to build RVs at daybreak

Araucana chickens won't lay eggs in captivity

Airplanes of roses lift above Quito mountains

Cultivated from crocuses in La Mancha, saffron suffuses my rice

Women cook circuit boards for gold flecks in Guiyu

You touch what I discard

Status updates stack up in Prineville warehouses

Data, coal-powered and far-flung

When fish diminish, folks find jobs in prisons

Sometimes children visit

Crouched on mounds of monitors, boys capture copper with magnets

Airplanes of microchips lift above Cascade mountains

Terminator seeds are hard to share

Bonfires burn motherboards into Agbogbloshie air

Sometimes children breathe it

And the fish diminish

The roses, the tea, and the edamame, far-flung

The roses, the tea, the microchips, and you

You breathe in what I disregard, friend

SONG FROM A BEACHED MUSIC BOX

FOR JESSI AT 6 & BEYOND

when I wear a dream coat
long with crumpled velvet
I'll umbrella you in the rain
warm you in the snow
and spread it on the sand when we picnic
in the ocean's neighborhood

near some small diner
where we'll seat some friends
we'll turn the booths to houses
hang lanterns from their doors

on one low blue table
we might try to grow some food
let's water with teacups, till with forks
& our food will feed the neighborhood

to our buttoned cuffs
we might pin straw and bendy flowers
that we'll name seven names
from an alphabet of Xs

when I have a chessboard to set in front of you
our queens will meet and delight each other
and they'll forget to play

when we hear three rainbows
sing like fifteen radios
when you ride a bike
with wheels that spin like suns
when you clap as fast
as flapping hummingbird wings
colors will croon for hours
in the flaming amber and its leaves

when you chat with mice
who animate the yard
you'll remind the sunflowers
to droop down their heads
so seeds and secrets fall

maybe we'll find a phone
on which to place a call
let's ring the trees next door
and tell them their shade is good

and let's stage a government
like a daily birthday party
where promises will be primroses
that wilt if they just aren't true
if we find five stop signs
to prop at any corners
we'll perimeter the Pentagon
mixing memos into songs

let's weave the bus lines
routed through our city
into woolen blankets
to warm the coldest slumber

and let's build a music box
to crank power for the city
to breach the dams and loose the salmon
and thank candles for their burning

thank candles for their burning
in this world of our making

let's make a world like that
as promising as primroses
blooming bright as hummingbirds
let's make a world like that

DEEP WATER HORIZON LEDGER

AT LEAST FIVE
GALLONS PER SECOND

In the time it takes me to say this, at least 40 gallons of oil will
have gushed out of the Deepwater Horizon site.
And now 50
And now 60
And now 70
And now 80 gallons of oil
In the time since this poem began, gushing out of the BP Deepwater Horizon
oil drilling site, I count 150 gallons of oil mixing into the Gulf of Mexico
saltwater.
And now 160
And now 170
And now 180
And now 190
And now 200
In the time since this poem began, I count 250 gallons rushing beyond the
failed concrete seal poured by Halliburton.
By this time tomorrow, at least 200,000 more gallons of oil will have leaked into
the Gulf of Mexico seawater. This, as I eat my eggs and scan the newspaper.
This, as I go on, burning oil BP drills for me each day, despite myself. This, as
each second, 5 more gallons of oil defy barriers and become the difficult ecology
of now.

Written 9:10–9:30 AM on May 4, 2010

AT LEAST TWENTY
GALLONS PER SECOND

In the time it takes me to say this, at least 160 gallons of oil will have gushed out
of the Deepwater Horizon site.
And now 200
And now 240
And now 280
And now 320 gallons of oil
In the time since this poem began, gushing out of the BP Deepwater Horizon oil
drilling site, I count 600 gallons of oil mixing into the Gulf of Mexico saltwater.
And now 640
And now 680
And now 720
And now 760
And now 800 gallons
In the time since this poem began, rushing beyond the failed concrete seal poured
by Halliburton, I count at least 1000 gallons of oil.
By this time tomorrow, at least 1.7 million more gallons of oil will have leaked
into the Gulf of Mexico seawater. This as we gather in a park in a city near the
Pacific, far from Gulf Coast, and near it, too. This, as I go on, burning oil BP drills
for me each day, despite myself, oiled ease. This, as each second, more than 20
gallons of oil defy barriers and become the difficult ecology of now.

*I have recorded and then updated this poem several times since the April 10 explosion of
the Deepwater Horizon oil rig. This iteration is at 10 AM on June 3, 2010.*

AT LEAST FOUR
GALLONS PER SECOND

In the time it takes me to say this, at least 32 gallons of oil will have gushed
out of the Deepwater Horizon site.
And now 40
And now 48
And now 56
And now 64 gallons of oil
In the time since this poem began, gushing out of the BP Deepwater Horizon
oil drilling site, I count 120 gallons of oil mixing into the Gulf of Mexico
saltwater.
And now 128
And now 136
And now 144
And now 152
And now 160 gallons
In the time since this poem began, rushing beyond the failed concrete seal
poured by Halliburton, I count at least 200 gallons of oil
By this time tomorrow, at least 300,000 more gallons of oil will have leaked
into the Gulf of Mexico seawater.
This as I near sleep in a city near the Pacific, far from Gulf Coast, and near it,
too. This, as I go on, burning oil BP drills for me each day, despite myself, oiled
ease. This, as each second, more than 4 gallons of oil defy barriers and become
the difficult ecology of now.

*This most recent iteration is at 10:30 PM on June 23, 2010: I used the lower
estimate released by National Incident Command's Flow Rate Task Force. I
converted into gallons—there are 42 gallons to a barrel—because it is easy for me
to imagine a gallon of milk, and even then, I subtracted the amount of oil that
BP is supposedly catching, using numbers from the Environmental News Service.
These numbers, then, are not an exaggeration; you can actually assume much higher
numbers. This poem reported much higher numbers (20 gallons per second) a few
weeks ago when none of the oil was caught.*

AT LEAST TWENTY GALLONS PER SECOND

In the time it takes me to say this, at least 160 gallons of oil will have gushed out of the Deepwater Horizon site.
And now 200
And now 240
And now 280
And now 320 gallons of oil
In the time since this poem began, gushing out of the BP Deepwater Horizon oil drilling site, I count 600 gallons of oil mixing into the Gulf of Mexico saltwater.
And now 640.
And now 680
And now 720
And now 760
And now 800 gallons
In the time since this poem began, rushing beyond the failed concrete seal poured by Halliburton, I count at least 1000 gallons of oil
By this time tomorrow, at least 1.7 million more gallons of oil will have leaked into the Gulf of Mexico seawater. This as type in a coffee shop in a city near the Pacific, far from Gulf Coast, and near it, too. This, as I go on, burning oil BP drills for me each day, despite myself, oiled ease. This, as each second, more than 20 gallons of oil defy barriers and become the difficult ecology of now.

BP removed the containment cap this morning from the Deepwater Horizon site, so now the oil is rushing out unchecked. I revised my poem-ledger at 10:45 AM June 23, 2010, to account for the abundant increase of oil.

In the time it takes me to say this sentence, BP
will have extracted more than
12 gallons of crude oil from the earth

and now 15
and now 18
and now 21
and now 24 gallons of crude oil

By this time tomorrow, BP will have
extracted more than 130,000 gallons of oil
from this earth.

and once coaxed into fuels, once burned

carbon rising from the fires, alchemy,
chemistry carbon joining to oxygen, oxygen

once coaxed into fuels and burned, the oil
BP extracts in a day will weigh down our
thickening atmosphere with more than 2
million pounds of carbon dioxide

As I speak these lines now, BP extracts oil
from the South China Sea, the North Slope
of Alaska, from Clair oilfield in the North Sea,
from Egypt, India, Azerbaijan, from the Ula
oilfield on the Norwegian Continental Shelf,
from the Rumaila oilfield in Iraq

and still, from deepwaters, from
deepwaters off Angola, from deepwaters
off Trinidad & Tobago, from the
deepwaters off Itaipú off Brazil

and still, from the deepwaters of the Gulf
of Mexico where millions of gallons of oil
sloshed and sloshes

among shrimp born eyeless to shrimp
born to shrimp alive when the Deepwater
Horizon exploded

among crabs born clawless to crabs
born to crabs alive when the Deepwater
Horizon exploded

It is difficult to sustain attention

on the oil, sloshing in the Gulf
on the oil, burning & rising &
thickening the air

This as I press my heels into the pebbled
beach of Brighton, looking south at the
English channel, far from the Gulf of Mexico,
but near it, too. This as BP purchases public
fondness, bending its logo into Olympic rings
in London. This as rain clouds rumple the sky,
while elsewhere, in the U.S, crops wither in
drought. This as we burn old & earthen algae
into a long-suffering climate.

Brighton, England, July 10, 2012

III

NOW STRIKE THIS BELL FOR SOUND

now strike this bell for sound
how sound circles out, to strangers

how a body quivers with sickness
how it quickens with life

whose bodies we grasp, whose eye glasses we match
whom we buy with our billfolds
who bilks a grandmother's trust
how fifty percent of bankruptcy is from medical bills
how we spin sickness on the roulette wheel of capital
catapaulting, catapaulting, catapaulting

how the lotto winner swore she'd never change
how gates & guards graft a neighborhood
who lives nearby who is not a neighbor
that person does not talk to that person
whose taxday is evasive
whose IRS envelope is annual and heavy

whose touch is infectuous
who hires a manucurist to feel a touch
whose home has what walls
who is sleepless in a pullout bed
whose park is a bedless sleep

who digs roots in dispossession
whose body sears from sugars
who survives

whose ashes fill rusted cans
who is not my enemy
whose global funeral finds its fans
whom I grieve for

who chased my car with his car
whom I escaped from
who I chase with my daily purchase
whom I will never know
who lives on an island receding to the sea

how a global wedding finds its fans
who is a boy who wishes to be glamorous
who is a girl who is a girl who is a girl
who is a girl

who names her truck 'snowball' and furies the
logging roads
whose teeth cut on smoke
whose teeth were pulled by a country doctor
who then moved to the city
who then moved his human body to the city
whose human face did not smile

who stands guard by the wrought iron the
barbed wire the chain link
who demands a callback

whose body is perfumed and sequined in the
burnished mirror
whose body is not claimed

who is not a mother but a cousin and a telemarketer
who is not a telemarketer when another job is offered
who is a mother and a telemarketer and a lover of tulips and tobacco

who is a sister is a brother is a brother to a brother to a brother to a
sister a sister a sister a brother

whose human body we recognize in its carbon in its sequins
that we recognize faces as beloved or we look down and keep walking

that we keep walking
who we grieve for
whose bodies we grasp
who is a suitor who suits us
whom we love whom we recognize
whom we love, unrecognized
that shape we strike for sound
whose bodies we claim

I DO NOT NEED TO LIVE EVERY MIRACLE

i.

The city blares with power lines & hidden TVs. I am comfortable today. I
do not need to live every miracle. A man was released from jail without his
wheelchair so he slid & crawled away but now he's back in jail, again & again,
for drinking a beer outside RiteAid & not indoors, hidden with TVs. A but-
terfly feeds on a sliced orange. Tender abdomen. Near-summer rain. 9-year-
old Jessi is crocheting beasts. Loves beasts, cat-beasts, bird-beasts, dog-beasts,
bug-beasts, rat-beasts, people-beasts. Growling awake, hungry for garden
grub, we beasts seem to do okay sometimes

ii.

Parched gardens, sweeping storms, sudden sun—clover's coming up & I'm
healing, I guess. Surgery is an injury to the body to make strange the body's
habits. Searing restart. The spy's son—pizza delivery, then espionage to pay
the family bills. My new neighbor digs a trench, readying a house for a family,
a baby to keep dry. What an effort each day is. Map of Spain on the table, a
book about donkeys, reverie in a pile. Green-throated hummingbirds thrum
among honeysuckle climbing toward the sun

iii.

Dim the door, the moon-musked want, the tree-deep, throat-loud, hand-
heaped want, the want for life, & the many who surround. Seven billion
hearts or so, I join you today & so on, alive like you, sun-bright blood, how
much we have in common, alive as we are, vocal chord tight, violins in the
night. The street light's burned out, & the woodpecker made a home in the
power pole. Hello, Good Night. I'll sleep for you again

ODE TO SLEEP

the sky shows where I am

some clock jammed at 4 a.m.

no need to destroy the stranger   life camped out in a body

bedfoam, crumbs of concrete   a backpack, moonlight

then a flashlight   heats up the night

now sleep is a bottle   smashed on a rock

shards snagged   by riptide

she is tired, she said   she is a fire in a cave of exposure

ticketed for sleeping   under the starry sky

the street a shapeshifter   for the sleepless

the river   a dragon of lights

the alley, gripped   by the hooves of a dumpter

dreams without sleep   are hallucinations says Ptery

o berry in a beak   ramshackled, seared

the body keeps on dreaming   disrobed of blanketed sleep

the street a shapeshifter   for the sleepless who spy

a fire of light on storefront glass   a phoenix divebombing the sea

she pays a fare to sleep   cheek pressed to bus glass

pigeons, husky-voiced, choral   roost in the eaves of a hotel

a million doors in this city

& here, side-by-side, doors fence sleep

so she may meander into wakefulness   rather than breaking awake

hello shadows moving on tent canvas   shadows lowering into sleep

o courage, the heart is a new wound   worn old with pumping

open the door between you & me   standing guard for each other

to dream within the shelter of sleep   the heart an old wound too—

no need to destroy the stranger   wartorn or at the next table or

sleeping on palettes   beyond the fence of doors

that gird uninterrupted sleep

& a right to dream, too—

for Ibrahim, Leo, Lisa, Ptery, & Tricia

LOTTO

*for the meatpacking
workers at Teamsters Local
557, who did find
power in numbers, at least
for a short victory*

to the open fields I told
A prophesy: poetic numbers came
Spontaneously

       —William Wordsworth

*"In the desperate lotto draw of
the "soul"(soul, a kind of out-
sourcing of the social) someone
wins a freedom dreamt of on the
iron mattress of finance"*

       *—Rodrigo Toscano, 12 Riddles
of Spirit, Crook in Hand*

telescoping mercuric
stars swollen with sight
& down here with bed-eyed
desire born-again opportunity
happy slot machine ring
up my music some numbers
cease to play but others
play on foreclosing what's
fast & steaded & near

I divine design deserve to

keep the numbers playing
out there in this america

12 fancies herself

a lotto dance
partner popular
as 1 as 1 as
9 likes 9 & wants
to marry him
with county courthouse
candied peace
oh 12 fancies herself
& 9 likes 9

5s think they've earned
their ease why this body
decided to be left-
handed

wealth is heritable
appears earned but

block party busting
neighbors move
away red-lined &

well then okay
well then

there's
always the
lottery

win win winning numbers
winsome numbers comely

come close small
buttons close my
blouse the sky is not
near this america
come close the present
is but a seizure
& the sky

too cluttered
for ufo spotting

come low by me
we will see
what we want to see

you know I am sincere
& in dynamic decay

highway 12
local 556
Tyson meat-
packing
plant Pasco

Washington

Mexican &
Bosnian & Sudanese &
Vietnamese workers

dull knives slam
down hard for cuts
that woman against
that cow so much
flesh hot & bloody & off
the small highway no signs
read Tyson no public tours

you will not face
restrictions in the job
market

the entire US
playing field yours
to explore

pay for our
services to increase
your chances

the easiest way
to America

a little luck

7s as white as
'naturalized' citizenship 1923

5s pray protestant & public
hate the 8s

penitent
union-minded stealing

gold in lunchpails
underdog landfill

graveside dollarstore
this house
my heritable wealth

my lucky number 2

the winning ticket
was sold
at 7/Eleven #14507
on SE 42nd

3 dead by gunfire
1 minimum 5 maximum
dead roadside bomb

outside & outside
& outside this is
an america

not a draft lotto

poor so willing

lightning striking
wind falling a roller
coaster pretty
penny pinching
fruit from a
tree water
shed sweep
stake

just my lucky
stars

three gunned down in a
barber shop one guard
killed by a bomb near
the polling station

I am 8 11 22 prime
mountains court
the train 7 courts
8 15 56 .875 not factorable
by 6

turning tricks behind
a curtain in the notions
shop lonely vitamin-less
homespun tricks
are extra turns exposed
light high the curtain low

today's lotto is a credit card
receipt blowing down an alley

I own this sequence
with dead identity

I dyed my hair squinted
wore glasses claimed
my winnings fixed
myself to look
like a winner like
the woman on this
identity card

squeezing auburn
my hair wet
& darker who
I must be
to place a lien
on the numbers
foreclose someone
else's lotto

is it demanding things?

pretty landscape plundered
all I have these small
buttons this blouse
opens up
touch your fingers
there

new millionaire
mimic close my cash register
worries

a poem is the numbers
as a man rides
a commuter train plays
the birthday of a daughter
who is outside out
there far as stars &
numbers trees & the
west out there
the lottery his lot a lost

daughter numbers
numbers rhyming numbers

that the winning ticket
might be in the woods with
a hunter who doesn't
know he's rich was
a favorite theory

so if I ask any woman out
now is she going to say yes?

I hope it's someone who
really needs it. it's too much
for one person to have

either slow down the line
or pay us more money

fast fast & lax
lacerations
workers of the world
more likely to die
the nurse says you're fine
on the kill
floor

& outside & outside
affluence of wine
tasters the 6s
with our riches
can't be stopped
by external costs

5 is a bland
soul gated
into riches

gone under
to plunder then
to plant

to plunder then
to plant trees

if everyone could win the lottery
pool of players pool of winners

another lotto
winner lodged
without bail
in the county jail

a lighthouse at sea
inurning thousands
of lotto winners

clock-in clock
out lotto winners
schlep the cannery
slush

lotto winners lotto winners
our populace brilliant with
billionaires canning
salmon cleaning
beef stooped repetitive
torsos twisted brilliant
billionairedom

I am your friend
clandestine
& on the clock

lovely numbers
you need not add up
for me you only need to be

1 at random
2 by work
3 a marriage
4 heaped perks
5 by family
6 decreed
7 eventual
8 thoroughly thieved

see the winners they want us see
a financial fix

cluttered sky informative

archival overexposed

burnt with stars

hope big enough to populate
the town where one winner
must live

hope as big as a
humvee an
astrodome

the lot of luck
is a lot of differentiation

tenement sun
is not is
the same sun
beachfront sun shantytown sun
vista view sun reservation sun
company town sun suburban sun
encampment motel underpass
gated community sun &
moon & planetarium

casting lots
a community chest
for one winner
yes like taxes but
winnowed to
one

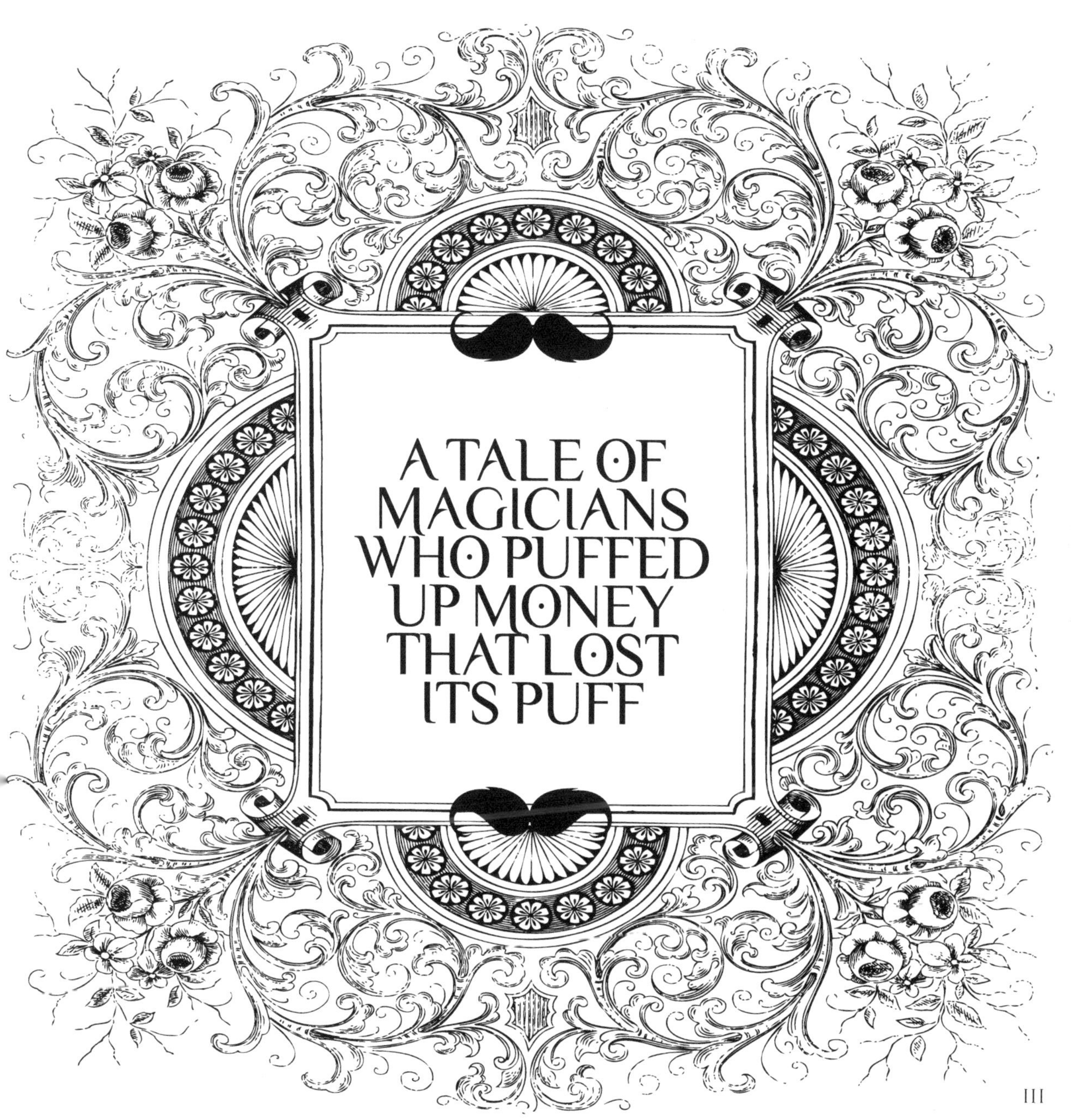

A TALE OF
MAGICIANS
WHO PUFFED
UP MONEY
THAT LOST
ITS PUFF

cast
Magician
Magician's assistant
Storyteller

props
Magician's hat, expanding flowers, chattering teeth, slide flute, gun with "bang" flag, flash paper, rubber chicken, stiff dog leash harnessed to an invisible dog named Roscoe, two-sided hand mirror, retractable knife, two-way water-squirting camera, toy crocodile, rabbit, magical picture book, paper money in assorted sizes, money bag, seagull-winged water drinking glass, rubber egg, chicken egg, coins (chocolate?)

These are suggested props based on the magic of the Magnificent Mitchelli, but please adapt according to your magician's repertoire. All music is based on the whistling talents of the Magnificent Mitchelli. Script is written conforming to the genders of performers in the premiere performance.

{low lights}

Magician whistles the Skaters' Waltz. Storyteller is perched on high stool with Giant Book titled "A Tale of Magicians Who Puffed Up Money that Lost its Puff"

There were once many Magicians who knew how to give money a little puff.

Magician sends sparks from a ring.

{raise lights}

People all over the country bought houses and houses and houses, but really, they could have bought roses and roses and roses

Magician plucks flower from the air.

or canaries and canaries and canaries.

Magician whistles like chirping bird.

It didn't really matter to the Magicians, as long as they could get the money to puff up greatly.

Not just anyone could puff up money quite like that.

It took magic, and a special magic where Magicians convince people they are seeing something that doesn't really exist.

Magician begins extended sequence while whistling Skaters Waltz, including walking an invisible dog, pulling flowers out of an empty bag, stiffening a rope, performing an optical paper illusion ("which one is larger?"), coughing up a red scarf, performing 'butterfly fantasy,' and levitating his own leg.

After all, in this particular story, with this particular cast of Magicians, most didn't make money off actual houses—those shelters where people stay dry from the elements. Instead, Magicians made money puff from a circus of bets about money people promised to pay to keep those houses.

Sometimes, now, looking back at the puffy money, the storms of money brushing against the shutters of all those shelters, sometimes now you might hear voices in television boxes, saying "all those people making promises on all those shelters, all those people are the problem with the economy today."

And we might imagine thousands of IOUs—those mortgages—dripping ash in the fire. And we might look at some of those promises, those IOUs and think, what wacky, dreadful promises. After all, some people were trying to puff up money by flipping houses like pancakes on a griddle, but they weren't the real Magicians, they weren't trying to puff money from nothing, they still needed a real house with maybe a door and some windows.

If all those promises powdered like ashes in the fire, if all those mortgages had gone bad, well, this economy wouldn't have smashed like Humpty Dumpty wobbly on a wall.

Magician plays slide flute.

No. The Magicians puffed up money to a puff at least ten times the amount of all those promises, those IOUs, those mortgages,

Magician pulls out money that gets bigger and bigger.
and when all those Magicians found out that their puffy money lost its puff, that's when the banks lost their puff, and all the king's horses and all the king's men put some of those banks back together again. Or rather, we did.

But that's getting ahead of the story.

You might ask just how the Magicians puffed up money to quite that puff.

<u>Reveal your magic tricks, Magician!</u> *{Storyteller & Magician's Assistant say in unison}*

Magician lights flash paper on chopsticks. Magician tosses coins into the audience.

Well, if we had a sack full of houses, thousands and thousands of houses, and smashed them up and shook the bag, we might piece them back together into a bunch of Frankenstein houses. Only, when the Magicians did this, they didn't worry about the houses (which could have been tulips or wheat or the air we breathe)
Magician raises tulip plant from behind box

they just took all those promises, those IOUs, and shook those in a bag, and cut them up and made Frankenstein mortgages, called "securities," or more specifically in this case, where they added all kinds of funny tricks like insurance for default, Collaterized Debt Obligations.

And then they piled those risky smashed up mortgages into "tranches"

Magician offers a branch

No, not branches. I said …. tranches.

Magician offers the branch again. Storyteller looks frantically toward the Magician's Assistant, who says "tranche" with a French accent and a suddenly donned beret.

But even though the Magicians borrowed a French word for slice that lent a bit of finesse, they mostly talked about those tranches like levels, like stories in a building, where the bottom level might protect the higher ones. And that bottom tranche was one place in the story where it gets really hazardous, like a sky of dragons or moat with crocodiles

Magician swims a toy crocodile through the air.

These bundles of chopped up mortgages, well, folks called them "toxic waste." But since we have a lot of metaphors flying around, let's not get too into that metaphor of ecological destruction, because really, what we're talking about are mortgages that people could barely pay.

Magician does a duck call.

People could barely pay these mortgages because so many were just so foul. What the Magicians needed were lots and lots of mortgages, lots and lots of people buying of houses, and it didn't matter if the people could afford the deals they signed.
Wild deals, deals that had exploding arms

Magician first explodes a party favor then shoots a gun with a bang flag.
Mortgages that became too crazy expensive, sky high into impossibility, like more than all the money than the amount the people brought home from their job, if they had a job. Or there were the negative amortizing mortgages, where people got

further and further behind, like someone trying to run to the next town on a treadmill strapped to a go-cart rolling backwards.

And if a person couldn't pay that mortgage, a banker wasn't looking down the street at a neighbor who would lose her home. Instead, lots of Magicians were waving wands around bits of the mortgage

Magician taps wand against mortgage.

and who knew who owned what anymore.

And really, who knows who owns what anymore, now that the banks are trying to grab back those millions of houses. The banks have to grab them whole, not doors to some houses and shutters to others, but since that's how they owned them, or sold them through those collatorized debt obligations, it's all rather confusing. And now the paperwork is fluttering, fortune cookie flimsy, and some banks hired some people to sign names rapid-fire to papers foreclosing on the houses, without reading all the words and the phrases, and it's all rather dodgy and shoddy and shammy.

Really, stay tuned to that story, which is still being written,
but back to the magic tricks—

Magician pulls out chattering teeth & a snake from a cup.

Magic tricks that also involved bunches of AAAs that ratings agencies dashed across the tranches, like frantic school teachers with frantic pens grading papers in a house of mirrors. And folks and governments all over the world thought, what a high grade that is! A great place to stash money, people's pensions and such.

And of course, the Magicians learned to make lots of money by charging fees for every which thing.

Magician begins pulling coins out of ears of people in the audience. Magician's Assistant follows with a money bag. Magician toys with audience, offering coins but quickly snatching them back.

It's like they sold tickets, not just for the show, but also, every magic trick, and not just every magic trick, but every gesture, every sword brandish, everything. Fees fees fees.

Well, the Magicians knew that they could only puff up money so much by owning bits of real houses, albeit fragments of titles scotch taped together, in a way. They could puff up money much, much more, if they were buying lots of other invisible things, too.

Velcro a magic trick called the Credit Default Swap onto the Collaterized Debt Obligations—and sleight of hand over sleight of hand—you have the Synthetic Collaterized Debt Obligation, which also meant placing bets on whether folks' mortgages would go bad.

Talk about trading in ill-will.

Folks could bet without owning anything, like betting that a house in the next town would blaze into flames one day.

Magician lights flash paper on a spoon.

Or if we were talking about walking dogs, which is a good sort of exercise and job for some, our Magician wouldn't be walking his dog named Roscoe, but his invisible dog named Roscoe,

Magician walks Roscoe, the Invisible Dog.

and wait, he'd be walking that invisible dog named Roscoe in a mirror, and sometimes, all we would see would be a mirror of a mirror of a mirror.

Magician's Assistant holds up a two-sided mirror. Then he begins to twirl it.

Because endless amounts of synthetic collaterized debt obligations could be created.

And talk about puff. The Magicians puffed up the money way *{storyteller reads on as Magicians holds up giant money}* beyond anything anyone paid toward a mortgage. And these Synthetic Collaterized Debt Obligations were so make-believe that they didn't even show up on the accounting ledgers. All they did was show up enough to crash the economy.
But there are a couple of plot details I forgot to mention.

Join me, if you will, in the spring of 2004, in a basement of the Securities Exchange Commission. The Securities Exchange Commission used to tell the Magicians that they couldn't puff up money to more than 12 times its size. This was called the net capital rule, and it had been around since 1975, but again, come springtime 2004, the commissioners said, okay, you Magicians can puff up money to 30 times its size. They cheered on that puff, and the big banks took a bow and maybe said thank you.

Magicians plays horn with whistle at the end.

As long as I tell that part of the story, I might as well back up more. Let's gaze toward 1999, that millennial cusp, when Congress repealed the Glass-Steagall Act.

Magician flies a drinking glass with seagull wings across the room.

No, not glass seagull. Glass-Steagall.

The Glass-Steagall Act *{storyteller wags a finger at the Magician who is beginning to fly the Glass Seagull across the room again. Magician shrugs}* had been around since 1933 to keep the Magicians from running into all the banks to puff up money. They were supposed to stay in their Puff Palaces, the investment banks, and away from commercial banks. But in 1999, down that came, and the Magicians came running into the commercial banks with their wands and their hats *{Magician touches wand to hat to pull out rabbit}* happy to have so many more props to play with, like mortgages that could get shook up in a bag.

And we know from our story that so many mortgages were foul, even though the Magicians said that lots of folks could pay, lots of folks couldn't, because people aren't made of money, they can't conjure it from the air no matter how many hours they work at the factory or bakery or phone bank or IT office or HR department or wherever. And the next year, with the Magicians roaming freely between their palaces and the government buildings, Congress passed the Commodity Futures Modernizations Act—with incantations to block any regulations on these magic tricks.

Perhaps the story is foreshadowed in the words we use, since words like mortgage, and amortizing, which describes what mortgages do, are rooted in 'mort,' which comes from the word 'death,' as in 'mortality'—

Magician stabs Magician's Assistant with retractable knife.

and while we're at, the 'fin' in 'finance' is like that too, as in 'finished,' 'final.' And that's what happened to so many mortgages, and all the puff around them, finished, final—kaput. It turned out the Magicians could only conjure money for so long, for what tale am I telling you?

Storyteller closes book & traces finger under title as audience says title. If children are in the front row, this can be directed toward them.

Yes. And the money lost its puff. And this economy smashed maybe not like Humpty Dumpty wobbly on a wall, but like the Magician recklessly smashing ol' Humpty Dumpty hard {Magician's Assistant throws egg against the wall, smashing it} and all the people's government and all the people's taxes rushed to fix the banks again.

And cash oozed into the Puff Palaces, those big banks, and those Magicians said they would lend more out, they said they saw us, beckoned to all of us—

Magician gestures to take someone's picture. A volunteer nods. Magician squirts her in the eye.

But the Magicians mostly stashed money in the palaces, and passed it among each other like birthday presents every day, because as a condition of their bailout, which they mostly wrote, they didn't have to account for how they spent the money. Meanwhile, people got poorer.

Again and again, the Magicians tell us that this new Congressional law or financial trick or whatever will help everyone out.

Magician gestures for person to take his picture. Hands the camera over. Person gets squirted in the eye again.

and they keep the money to grow their profits,

and this just seems to happen again and again.

If the Magicians keep us believing in their made-up world, where lots of numbers and phone calls and first class flights equals value, they'll puff up money around lots of other real things, like water or wheat or tulips

Magician grows flowers from his hand.

or the air we breathe.

Storyteller closes book & approaches crowd.

Today I've told a tale of magic tricks, a killjoy tale, a sinister
tale of lousy magic—

But this is an evening tale, and the sky is dark and we're easing toward sleep, so
let's wish for the Magicians we would queue up to see

Wouldn't we queue up for a magic that refused reckless profits for the few, that
concerned itself with the many in this world?

Wouldn't we queue up for a magic conjured so that all people, and the ecosystems we
are among, are what flourish. Now that's a magic I'd like.

A magic that makes shelters for all, not mansions for a few. Now that's a magic I'd like.

Because the Magicians of finance seem to have written most people out of their story.

Magician flutters book with blank pages.

But we need a magic that pictures us, too—

Magician flutters book with pages drawn.

And pictures us vividly.

Magician flutters book again, with colored pictures.

<u>We'd like a magic like that. {Storyteller & Magician's Assistant say in unison}</u>

*Magician lights flash paper in a rubber chicken's mouth, and, after the flame
shoots out, tosses the chicken into the audience.*

Exit.

Magician whistles the Skaters Waltz.

BEWARE THE FURY

Beware the fury of the financier

rote fury, puffy money, bankers who bank

on diverted attention. Divested

power. I attend to a kestrel

showing its shadow to the morning floor.

My neighbor's crusy music. My daughter's

trusty lemur doll. A train, sooty &

passing four stories below. Power.

This is a sentence about synthetic

collaterized debt obligations:

a bit of what gets lost in the paper

shuffle of profit. Doorway to a shelter.

Roof sloped to slide rain. Bankers, bilking

aplenty—I'm riveting my attention now.

NOTES ON THE LIVES OF SOME POEMS THUS FAR

A poem might be read as though it has a "long biography," accruing meaning through shifting contexts, Peter Middleton suggests in his book *Distant Reading*; I have taken this notion to heart as a writer with an interest in recasting poems. The following notes attend to the publication histories of the poems as well as performance, material, and social histories. In some cases, I include brief political contexts, with the hope that some poems might carry contexts forward, like burrs caught in fur. I document various iterations of these poems on my website: kaiasand.net

The President Probably Talks was first published in *Tinfish Magazine*. McSweeney's press included it in two publications: *The McSweeney's Book of Poets Picking Poets* as well as *The Poetry Chains of Dominic Luxford in the Three Books Held Within By Magnets*. (Thank you to Rodrigo Toscano who tagged me in the McSweeney's poetry chain and to Dominic Luxford who created these two volumes). Brandon Shimoda recorded a soundcast of this poem for the Wave Books PoetryPolitic project in 2008, which is now archived on the PennSound online repository of audio poetry.

Air the Fire
I wrote *Air the Fire* (as well as *So He Raised His Hand*) as part of The Watcher Files Project, an investigation of surveillance documents the Portland Police Bureau collected on civic and activist groups in the 1960s, 70s, and 80s. After the Oregon legislature ruled in 1981 that it was illegal for the police to surveil activists not under criminal investigation, the files were slated to be destroyed. Winfield Falk, the Portland police detective who created many of the surveillance files, stole the files and stashed them in a barn. Found two decades later,

they were anonymously delivered to the *Portland Tribune* newspaper, and then city archivists fought successfully for public access to the files. The Watcher Files was an artistic collaboration with Garrick Imatani, with whom I shared an artist residency at the City of Portland Archives and Records Center from 2013-2015, a public art commission by the Regional Arts and Culture Council. We documented this project at looseleafservices.us

Grappling with the exposure of activists through police surveillance, Imatani and I posed a question to each other: "where is anonymity within a public record?" *Air the Fire* is my response. I embroidered these poems as three black panels, nearly five feet long each, black mercerized cotton thread on black linen. My choice of these materials was guided by our inquiry into illegibility and legibility, anonymity and exposure.

I exhibited *Air the Fire* in windows at the Multnomah County Library North Portland Branch, the Portland State University Academic & Recreation Center, and the PDX Contemporary Gallery Window Project. Now the poems are exhibited in the boardroom of the Regional Arts and Culture Council as part of the City of Portland's portable collection of public art. Working with Amanda Hendricks and Jonathan Raissi, Imatani and I also translated these poems into sound performances at The New Structure performance series through Project Cityscope at the Shout House in Portland; the Northwest Archivists 2014 Conference in Spokane; the Multnomah County Library North Portland branch; and Portland State University. Some images can be found here: http://kaiasand.net/watcher/

So He Raised His Hand
After reading police surveillance reports on Lloyd
Marbet's activism, Garrick Imatani & I traveled to
land Lloyd caretakes north of Estacada, Oregon to
learn some of his stories of dogged activism to help free
Oregon from nuclear power plants, both through the
demolition of Trojan nuclear plant and the prevention
of additional plants such as the Pebble Springs Nuclear
Plant. I arranged seven of these stories onto the page,
adding verses based on his images and rhythms. I wrote
opening and closing poems that cast Lloyd as "the
Caretaker." Lloyd edited all of the text.

Inge Bruggeman created a letterpress edition of this poem,
which was exhibited as part of the Antena Exhibit at the
Blaffer Gallery in the University of Houston; Multnomah
County Library North Portland Branch; the Portland
State University Academic & Recreation Center; and
the Cascade Gallery at Portland Community College. I
have performed these poems with many people, in venues
such as the Switch Reading Series; the City of Portland
Archives and Records Center; Cascadia Poetry Festival
at Seattle University; Department of English Visiting
Writer Series at Washington State University (The Bell
Tower); and University of Alabama, Tuscaloosa (Jemison
Mansion). Thank you to all who have taken the stage with
me to give Lloyd's stories voice. Some images are archived
here: http://kaiasand.net/watcher/

Tiny Arctic Ice
As a daunted human creature of this world, I write
down its details, a poetic accounting. *Tiny Arctic Ice* is
an experiment in recasting: I wrote the first version of
the poem in 2007 when I built a book out of a teabag
for the Dusie Kollektiv. I recast it through performance

in 2009 at Cabaret Voltaire in Zurich, Switzerland,
curated by Susana Gardner; Swiss poet Katherin
Schaeppi helped me translate lines into Swiss that we
jotted onto paper airplanes Jessi Wahnetah and Stella
Gockenbach launched into the crowd. I also handed
out flowers wrapped in lines of the poem in 2009 at
the Market Day Poetry Series, St. Johns Book Store
in Portland, Oregon; recast the poem as an accordion
structure built from the *Financial Times* newspaper in
2012 for the Hi Zero poetry reading series in Brighton,
England; and performed it as tangled e-waste at the
Ecopoetics Conference at Berkeley.

This poem has been published in *Alive at the Center*
(Ooligan Press, 2013); *Big Energy Poets: Ecopoetry Thinks
Climate Change*; and *Capitalism, Nature, Socialism*; as
well as *Dusie Kollektiv* edition of *Jacket Magazine*. Mel
Nichols created a letterpress pamphlet of *tiny arctic ice*,
alongside a poem by Semezdin Mehmedinović; and Jim
Dine turned the text into one of his *Hot Dream* books
(Steidl Editions, 2008).

I will continue to recast this poem, accruing details. The
sum is elusive, abundant. It spills over the form. Some
images: http://kaiasand.net/tiny-arctic-ice/

Song from a Beached Music Box
This poem was published in *Primary Writing*, edited by
Phyllis Rosenzweig and Diane Ward; and *Kindergarde:
Avant-Garde Poems, Plays, Stories, and Songs for Children*,
edited by Dana Teen Lomax (Black Radish, 2013), which
also posted a recording of the poem on the Black Radish
Press webpage.

Deep Water Horizon Ledger
During the months of May & June 2010, I performed
this poem on a walk I led in North Portland as well as
at a poetry reading in Director Park in downtown Port-
land, and it was published on *PoMotion Poetry* and *Poets
for Living Water*. The poem served as breaking news,
my up-to-the-minute (more or less) accounting of the
oil spill. *Pocket Notes* (Fall 2012) published the notes I
jotted toward the poem's postscript.

Now Strike that Bell for Sound
Under an earlier title (*bell curve*), this poem was pub-
lished in the *Ixnay Reader* edited by Jenn & Chris Mc-
Creary. I first performed this at the Walla Walla Poetry
festival curated by Charles Potts and Travis Catsull.

I Do Not Need to Live Every Miracle
I wrote these poems, later published in *Summer Stock*, for
an Allen Ginsberg tribute event at the Elizabeth Leach
Gallery in Portland.

Ode to Sleep
Ode to Sleep is dedicated to Lisa Fay, Ibrahim Mubarak,
Ptery Poul Lieght, Leo Rhodes, and Tricia Steele Reed,
some of the organizers at Right 2 Dream Too, a direct
action that commenced in 2011 at the same time the
Occupy Portland encampment settled about ten blocks
south and equidistant from the Willamette River.
Seasoned organizers, they seized the opportunity opened
up by a private property owner disgruntled with the city
government, accepting his offer to lease the land for a
place for people who live without shelters to sleep. I have
been fortunate to work with Mubarak and Rhodes on
other poetry projects, and I admire their creativity for
justice, their poetics of action. Through self-governance,

Right 2 Dream Too has endured for nearly six years, and
was awarded a lease to city land for the next ten years. I
have learned so much from them, including facts about
sleep deprivation and its health effects for people who
live on the streets.

Lotto
In 2005, workers at the Tyson meatpacking plant in
Pasco Washington were in a fight to retain their union,
Teamsters Local 556. Many people in the nearby town
of Walla Walla supported these efforts, but had little
access to the workers, who labored in an unmarked
plant off the highway. When students and community
members gathered to hear *Fast Food Nation* author Eric
Schlosser speak at Whitman College, Jules Boykoff and
I photographed audience members holding up messag-
es they wrote on signs for the workers. Then, at a rally
in Pasco, we photographed workers holding messages
in which they wrote why a union was important. We
delivered the photos back and forth to attempt to build
solidarity. Faces, words, handwriting—telegrams of a
sort. This was one small action within a large campaign
for the union that, despite extraordinary leadership, was
ultimately defeated. I was fortunate to think about how
poetry and art might contribute to a labor campaign,
and I thank in particular Paul Apostolidis for creating
that space.

I wrote *lotto* while I worked on that labor effort. While
the poem investigates the American dream, green card
lotteries, and military draft lotteries, that labor campaign
in Walla Walla courses through the poem. *Lotto* was then
published as a wee book handmade by Susana Gardner
for Dusie Books; and in *Tool: A Magazine* edited by Eric
Sweet. Jim Dine used the text for one of his books in his

Hot Dreams series (Steidl editions, 2008). Sources for the poem include "A Secret Worth $340 Million: One Mystery Powerball Winner Strikes It Rich in Jacksonville" (*The Oregonian*, October 21, 2005); "Blood Sweat & Fear: Workers' Rights in U.S. Meat & Poultry Plants" (Human Rights Watch Report, 2005); "Powerball Winners Rebut Story on List of Demands" (Associated Press, Medford, Ore. November 12, 2005); Iraq Body Count (www.iraqbodycount.org); "Trouble Trails Winner of $1 Million Prize." (Katy Muldoon, *The Oregonian*, October 29, 2005, B3) as well as various state lottery sites and various websites offering paid assistance with the green card lottery.

A Tale of Magicians Who Puffed up Money that Lost its Puff

Early in the fall of 2010, Jules Boykoff, our daughter Jessi Wahnetah, and I visited whistler and magician Mitch Hider in Eugene, Oregon, where he whistled as a human jukebox in his driveway, then staged a magic show in his living room. Afterward, we brainstormed ideas for creating a magic show to tell the story of the deceitful shenanigans surrounding the 2008 financial collapse. Over the next couple of months, I wrote a script, mailing drafts to Mitch, and we talked by phone, dreaming up magic tricks to intersect with the script, editing the script to engage the magic. All the while, Jules provided feedback. Aiming to describe finance with playful language, I frequently read the script to then eight-year-old Jessi, with her keen ear for delight and rhythm.

On December 1, 2010, we performed the show at Field Work, a temporary art space in downtown Portland, Oregon that inhabited a former retail space slated for demolition (it is now demolished and replaced by con-dominiums). I played the role of storyteller, Mitch performed the magician known as the Fabulous Mitchelli, and Jules served as the Magician's Assistant. Jessi organized children's participation from the audience, and Jen Coleman was an audience volunteer. Susan Schoenbeck and Jessi created props. The magic show was part of a larger Econ Salon, a format I began curating in 2008 by bringing together poets, artists, economists, and activists to better understand the financial collapse and organize creative responses. This Econ Salon also featured Ibrahim Mubarak, who discussed his experiences of homelessness; Angela Martin, who discussed organizing people around debt; and installations by David Buuck and Jennifer Hardacker, as well a dollhouse squat by the direct-action organization, Right 2 Survive. Video footage of the premiere performance is available at: http://kaiasand.net/happy-valley-project/Rob McLennan published *A Tale of Magicians Who Puffed Up Money that Lost its Puff* as an above/ground press chapbook in 2013.

Beyond the Fury

I embroidered *beyond the fury* on an eight-foot dropcloth while I read books on finance: this poem was my material translation of abstract information. My grandmother and mother, Marjorie Pratt and Meg Eberle, who taught me to embroider when I was a child, embroidered some letters on the poem, and Jessi dotted "i"s with French knots. *Beyond the fury* was exhibited at Sandy 23 when David Abel curated Object Poems in 2011; and at the Dusie Poetry Group Exhibit in the Brown University Library, Providence, Rhode Island, in 2015. During Occupy Portland in 2011, I read it into the People's Microphone at a rally on the waterfront, the lines echoing through many voices of the human mic.

More thanks

I am grateful to many, many people who provided opportunities for me to realize these poems, including David Abel, Diana Banning, Israel Bayer, Jane Beebe, Joel Bettridge, Devin Busby, Kristin Calhoun, Kathy Carbone, Cathryn Chudy, Marti Clemmons, Alicia Cohen, Jen Coleman, Sandra Comstock, Anna Daedalus, Jeremy Okai Davis, Jim Dine, Donald Dunbar, Amy Fackler, Ann Marie Fallon, Carolyn Forché, Kent Ford, Susana Gardner, Robert Duncan Gray, the late Michelle Greenblatt, Jamalieh Haley, Mary Hansen, Jared Hayes, Pamela Hickman, Jen Hofer, Brian Johnson, Max Johnson, Hank Lazer, Sam Lohmann, Joe Luna, Dominic Luxford, Nadine Antoinette Maestas, Paul Maziar, Diana Michener, Pattie McCarthy, Caitlin Moore, Andrea Murray, Paul Nelson, Joanne Oleksiak, Shin Yu Pai, Jenifer Park, Jonathan Penton, J.P. Pluecker, Deborah Poe, Amy Powell, Kristin Prevallet, Nora Quiros, Jimmy Radosta, Néna Rawdah, Joan Retallack, Leo Rhodes, Crystal Rodgers, Katy Rossing, Linda Russo, Sandy Sampson, Tim Shaner, Kristen Sheeran, Brandon Shimoda, the Sisters of Loretto, Teresa Tamiyasu, Stacey Tran, Elizabeth Treadwell, Kevin Varrone, Mark Wallace, Heather Watkins, Marie Watt, Patricia Welch and Leni Zumas.

Allison Cobb and I have regular conversations about investigative poetics. She offered me important feedback on this book.

Thank you to Carolyn Forche and the Lannan Center for Poetics and Social Practice at Georgetown for opportunities to discuss this work.

I am so grateful to Jeff Sanner for his thoughtfulness with this design. He was generous and patient and collaborative, inventing this form to recast these poems anew. These poems have been out in the world, some for a decade, so herding them into book-form was quite a task.

And I am deeply grateful to Susan Schultz, who gives so much of her heart, her smarts, and her time to the culture work of poetry.

I have the gift of a supportive and large family, and while I am naming but a few, I am supported by many. My 91-year-old grandmother Marjorie Pratt is as close to a muse as anyone could hope for, and my aunt Nancy Neet wheels her all around town to make sure she can be present at my readings. My niece Callista Smith engages me in thoughtful conversations about art. Neal Sand demonstrates the capacity to view life delightfully askew and with integrity. Susan Schoenbeck offers loving support and enthusiasm for each new poem. Meg Eberle is my comrade in writing, her warmth and strength and zest coursing along life's vicissitudes. Jessi Wahnetah is daughter extraordinaire, whose heart and ear and wit help me grow as a poet and a person. We chat in call-&-response wordplay, a poetics of the everyday. Jules Boykoff is my beloved partner: we tend our hearth to engage the world, more than two decade deep together in our attempt at living with open hearts and humor and a hope that our care for language might join well with our concern for social justice.

Also available from TinFish Press:

Lissa Wolsak, *Of Beings Alone*, 2016

Jonathan Stalling, *Lost Wax: Translation Through the Void*, 2015

Lynn Young, *Where's My Ritspick?* 2015

Albert Saijo, *WOODRAT FLAT.* 2015

Norman Fischer, *Escape This Crazy Life of Tears* (Japan, July 2010). 2014

Donovan Kūhiō *Colleps, Proposed Additions.* 2014

Lehua M. Taitano, *A Bell Made of Stones.* 2013

Steve Shrader, *The Arc of the Day | The Imperfectionist.* 2013

J. Vera Lee, *Diary of Use.* 2013

Jack London is Dead: Contemporary Euro-American Poetry in Hawai'i (and Some Stories),
edited by Susan M. Schultz. 2012

Ya-Wen Ho, *last edited [insert time here].* 2012

Maged Zaher, *The Revolution Happened and You Didn't Call Me.* 2012

Jai Arun Ravine, แล้ว *and then entwine.* 2011

Elizabeth Soto, *Eulogies.* 2010

Kaia Sand, *Remember to Wave.* 2010

Daniel Tiffany, *The Dandelion Clock.* 2010

Paul Naylor, *Jammed Transmission.* 2009

Lee A. Tonouchi, *Living Pidgin: Contemplations on Pidgin Culture*, 2nd edition. 2009

Lisa Linn Kanae, *Sista Tongue*, 2nd edition. 2008

Meg Withers, *A Communion of Saints.* 2008

Hazel Smith, *The Erotics of Geography.* 2007

Linh Dinh, *All Around What Empties Out.* 2003, [out of print]. Subpress/Tinfish

Caroline Sinavaiana-Gabbard, Alchemies of Distance. 2001, [out of print]. Subpress/
Tinfish/Institute of Pacific Studies

For other TinFish Press publications, including chapbooks and *TinFish* journals
1-20, visit our website: tinfishpress.com

In August 1940 when speaking of the pilots in the Royal Air Force who died preventing the German Luftwaffe from bombing Great Britain into surrender, Winston Churchill said: "Never was so much owed by so many to so few." We might say about Wall Street Bankers who brought on the Great Financial Crisis of 2008: "Never was so much damage done to so many by so few." In her collection of poems *A Tale of Magicians Who Puffed Up Money that Lost Its Puff* poet Kaia Sand holds up a mirror for us to see the many faces of humanity – financial destroyer, environment protector, nuclear power resister, future economy creator -- as only a poet can. Captivating literature and insightful politics are each hard to come by. Finding both in the same place is a rare jewel to be treasured and enjoyed.

—**Robin Hahnel**, Economist and author of *Economic Justice and Democracy: From Competition to Cooperation* (Routledge 2005) and *Of the People, By the People: The Case for a Participatory Economy* (AK Press, 2012).

Some of us inhale what others exhale. Kaia Sand's book reminds us of this simple fact. In this, a metaphor about love, daily life, community and power unfolds. These poems provide a tremendous answer to the question of what it means to be a poet who is deeply aware of those who live down river and down wind from power's malice. Deeply beautiful and tough, this is a book that is not only conscious of itself and of the world, it actually invites the reader to partake in this consciousness. It will make us meander into wakefulness.

—**Maged Zaher**, Author of *The Revolution Happened and You Didn't Call Me*

Kaia Sand's work always interests me: her inventories, interventions, recordings, dispatches, her *mixing memos into songs*, her soundings and measurements and exposés. These are lived poems, necessary and urgent and I learn from them. She is to be honored, read, shared, and given our undivided attention.

—**Carolyn Forché**, Author *Blue Hour* (HarperCollins, 2004) Editor, *Against Forgetting: Twentieth-Century Poetry of Witness* (W. W. Norton, 1993).